Lessons from the Crawl Space

How to Find Hope in Life's Dark Places

By Amy Johnson

Cover Art by Jeanne Marie Decklar

Acknowledgments

Setting out to write a book that dives deep into your past and exposes huge parts of you is a daunting task. I want to say thanks to so many people who have supported me along the way. Thank you to my husband and kids for putting up with the emotional times when I was a bit of a wreck. Thanks to my in-laws for believing in me always. Thanks to those of you who read my book and told me you thought I could be a writer! Thanks Christina, Diana, Janice, and Meric, for reading, critiquing, and encouraging me. I love you guys.

Thanks to my mom and my sister for agreeing to let me share my story. It was your story too in some ways, and I am thankful that you allowed me to use the past for good! Thank you Jeanne for making this work of art called a book cover and for encouraging this dream of mine to empower those who need to see light in their own personal crawl spaces of life. Gigantically huge thanks to my sweet Maria for being my friend, my editor, my armor bearer, my sounding board, and my biggest fan on this journey and hopefully on the journeys yet to come.

Finally thanks to the One who brought me through it all! He is the One who gives me a reason to get up in the morning and a reason to push through each day. Thank you Lord for giving me purpose and teaching me these lessons from the crawl space.

I hope this book helps you find hope in your dark places. God bless you all. Thank you for reading.

Amy Johnson

Table of Contents:

Lessons from the Crawl Space: Prologue

Fear of man will prove to be a snare

But whoever trusts in the Lord is kept safe.

Proverbs 29:25

The space was dank and damp. It smelled of earth yet filled me with a peace that is hard to explain.

I can still picture the small box of books and the carpet bag full of small toys and strings. Things I used to make my little creations.

If I sit in a corner, close my eyes, and wrap my arms tightly around my legs, I can still go there. I can see it, smell it, feel it.

My refuge, my comfort in times of trouble, Jesus met me there in that little underground room. It was a crawl space under the wooden toy box in my room in the house where I grew up. Dirt floor, a few spiders, the smell of decaying earth—as an adult it seems uninviting. The thought of the cramped quarters makes it seem even more so. But to me that crawl space was camouflage; it was safety.

So, you may ask—

Why go back? Why would I want to? Why allow my mind to travel back to times of pain, fear, or terror? Is there a reason I would want to return to the nightmares of a five- to eight-year-old girl? Yes—

because by remembering the fear, I see clearly the face and hear clearly the voice of the One who saved me. Because to me that crawl space was hidden. It was a place of safety.

My hope as I fill these pages with the words of my life and the images of my heart, is that those who read these words will see hope in their situation. I hope that they will see light in the dark and beauty in the ashes, once light is exposed to that darkness, once the ashes are shaped by the hands of the Almighty God.

Everyone has a story, a way we got from point A to point B in our lives! I look at where I am in my life and I think, "Wow, God, you are truly amazing in how you took someone broken like me and used me. How you took the broken pieces of an ugly life and brought restoration to make a beautiful mess!"

As I begin to write the chapters in this book I hope to paint a picture of how God can take a broken life and restore it. How God can make beauty from the ashes of the burnt remnants of our lives. I will also explain to you how God did this for me, from the sketches I remember of the lessons I learned in the crawl space.

Chapter 1: *Tangible*

I remember the first time I saw the face of Jesus. I was seven years old. My father was having an episode, and when Dad was in a bad place, it was best not to be where he was. I sat in the space under my toy box, under the floorboard in my bedroom. And there I talked to Jesus face to face. He told me, "It is okay, my child. You're gonna be okay." And then I told a story to Jesus, about something fanciful I am sure, although I can't remember the details. He sat with me in my little space. He held my hand and I sat in his lap. Unbelievable? Maybe to you, but to me, Jesus was my life line. He was my friend. Jesus made me feel braver than I was. Jesus took a dirt floor and a drafty crawl space and turned it into my refuge.

To me Jesus became tangible. He was real!

The dictionary defines *tangible* as:

> *Something perceptible by touch; clear and definite; real*

To understand the stories you are about to read in this book, you first have to see where the story began.

My father was drafted into the United States Army when he was 18 years old. Nearly the moment he was drafted, he was selected to go into a special elite group of airborne soldiers called the Green Berets. This group of soldiers were then scooped up and flown to Vietnam, where they fought for their lives. They did and saw unspeakable things. Then when their tours in 'Nam were done, they came home. Many of them were broken in body, and others, like my father, broken in their minds and hearts!

Thus the story began of a family who, no matter how hard they tried, could just not get away from brokenness.

It is easy to look at our lives and be pulled into the drudges of the things that our pasts hold. It is a little harder to pull through and come out to a place in the story where we begin to believe that we are, in fact, going to make it. It is even more of a challenge still to come to a place in life after pain where we see hope, restoration, and healing, a place where we rise above the circumstances of our past, and begin to thrive.

I serve a tangible God! I have begun to see Him clearly and understand His provision for me. I have gotten a glimpse of His heart. I have also come to a place where my brokenness is no longer in the forefront of my life. Instead, the forefront of my life is displaying a picture of grace. This clear, present, and reachable God, with whom I am so deeply enamored, is the reason I have come to this place of wholeness. It is also the sole reason I can be in a place where I am capable of ministering to others.

As a pastor, I daily get glimpses of how broken people's lives are. I see many pictures of depression, fear, anger, anxiety, and dysfunction. I see broken people living their broken lives. However, there is a hope of having so much more joy and peace in our lives. With God's help, I can see a clear picture of protection and non-understandable peace in my own personal life. This is the grace that God gives me! Even though I still have times when sadness consumes me and fear grips me like duct tape, I know where to turn. I can turn to Jesus!

What would it mean for you to have a tangible God in your life? If you could really know that in the midst of your hardest times that you would never be alone, never be forsaken or forgotten? Would that change things for you?

How would that kind of real God inspire you to live your life differently?

Could you trust Him enough to know that even when things don't happen the way you think they should, that God still loves?

Having a tangible God has been my inspiration to show God's clear and definite love to others. A Love that is real. Love you can see, touch, and feel.

What does this mean? For me, it means...

I will be a listener

I will be a help

I will give to others

I will be present

I will pay attention

I will be a friend

I will be a bright spot in someone's darkness

I will sacrifice my own time when I see a need.

I will let God use my story.

I am not a person who trusts easily. Often when you are broken, you can close off the most intimate parts of yourself to others. We call it protection, or self-preservation. God has had to show Himself to me in some pretty real ways. He has proven Himself to be trustworthy. I believe that God is teaching me to follow Him in tangible, real ways!

Every time I hear from another that I have been a blessing to them, it is like God is speaking to my heart, telling me that I am on the right track.

I am driven by the knowledge that people are hurting. I am spurred on by the understanding that just maybe, my experiences can be a help. I find rest and peace in the undeniable fact that God can take pain, fear, loneliness, and sadness and turn them into something beautiful! I am a testimony of God's ability to turn ashes into beauty. My prayer is that God becomes tangible to you as well.

We all need a Savior and a Light in our darkness.

Psalms says:

The Lord is my light and my Salvation (27:1)

Whom do you turn to when life gets tough? When your friends are struggling, where do you lead them? I say, lead them to the One who is tangible! God is the answer. God is the hope. God is real.

Psalm 46:1 says:

God is our refuge and strength, a very present help in trouble.

Let God find you in your crawl space. He is the only real and tangible God.

Chapter 2: *Carefully and quietly*

I can remember the fear I felt, the desperate need to keep quite. I hear the shuffling sound as I lay in my bed. I must move carefully and I must be quiet. I was a strong six-year-old. Thank God for the muffling benefit of the brown fuzzy carpet in my bedroom. I knew I only had minutes to hide. I slid the toy box quickly but quietly, just enough to be able to lift the hatch. I had to be able to keep the door hidden. I believed with all my six-year-old heart that no one else knew about the hole in my closet floor but me, for not once did anyone ever find me there.

I would go to my hiding place carefully and quietly. I wouldn't wait around for anything scary or hurtful to find me. I would stealthily run to my place of refuge. I would not scream out or draw attention to myself but quietly run to my place of safety.

Just like there were times when I didn't feel safe out in the open as a child, it is a fact that this world we live in can be very unsafe for our hearts.

In a world of noise, media, and distractions, it is very easy to get caught up in the fast and noises of it all. Fast and noisy can be attractive. It can pull you into its fun, feel-good draw.

I often remember that carefully and quietly means to slow down and take time to clear my mind. To me, this means many things. First, it means learn to disconnect. If, as a child, I got distracted by things sitting on my shelves or if the toys inside my toy box were to grab my attention, the consequences would have been no fun at all. For those of you who know much about warriors with PTSD who experience lifelike hallucinations, you know if they think you are an enemy, they will treat you like an enemy. This was my fear. My crawl space provided a refuge where I could hide from my father's disillusioned reality.

When I saw the last of the gap close from my hole in the floor, a peace would come over me. I was safe.

What distractions in life keep us from turning to Jesus? I have learned that desperate times call for desperate measures. When desperate, we need to turn to Jesus—not run away from Him!

I am so easily distracted sometimes. Even while I am writing this chapter, I have walked the dog, collected the mail, changed the laundry, posted a picture of the snacks I am eating (yes, I know that is ridiculous), and checked emails, Facebook, and text messages 14 times each. But when it is time for my alone time with my God, I try to keep the distractions to a minimum. Why? Because, if my line to my refuge, my ever present help, is broken, I face consequences.

I have found that the times when I feel the most tempted, the times when I feel the saddest, and the times when I feel the loneliest, are the times when I feel the most distanced from God. The times when I give in to things I know I shouldn't are not usually immediately following a good devotion or while listening to my favorite worship station on Pandora. Quite the contrary! Those times come when I am distracted. When I lose my focus or when I focus on something negative someone said about me or my family. When someone hurts me, or I am having my own little pity party, I become wrongly focused. When my mind moves quickly and loudly I find it gets easier to deviate from the plan that God has in place for me.

Carefully and quietly! I have to remember. Do not run to the distractions. Run to the One who keeps me grounded. Run there and take the time to quiet my heart so I can hear what it is His still, small voice has to say to me!

The Lord will fight for you, you only have to be silent. (Exodus 14:14)

I find that when I can slow down and quietly put Christ in my mind, God takes over and it becomes much harder for me to keep wrong thoughts. That is the Lord fighting for me.

Carefully and quietly is a lesson I learned from my crawl space. I hope you learn the same lesson from yours.

Chapter 3: *Darkness cannot exist in the light*

As the last gap closed, I was no longer able to see moonlight—I was in total darkness. I would feel around the floor in the special place until my hand made contact with my flashlight. And as I turned it on, not only was there a feeling of "Eureka . . . and then there was light," but also the darkness had no choice but to disappear. Amazing— dark simply cannot exist when light is present. I have felt the reality of this more than once. I remember conversations I have had with my sons. They are amazing! They love Jesus by their own choice . . . because He is tangible to them. I specifically remember one conversation I had with them a couple years ago, when they first discovered what it feels like to be set apart—to be different from the other kids. I remember my oldest son telling me about how strange and sad it felt to walk into a room and see some of his friends all huddled and chatting about something and then have everyone shut up when he started to walk towards them.

"I hate it, Mom, why do they treat me like I'm weird?" He asked me. "I need friends too. I feel so alone. I only have one friend, Mom." It broke my heart for about 30 seconds. As I pulled my sweet son in for a hug, I asked him, "What do you think those boys were talking about?" "Well, probably girls or something." "Do you think their conversation was appropriate?" I asked. "Well, no, probably not," he said. I am all about the teachable moments of life, and here was a big one staring me right in the face! Darkness and light cannot exist together, and dark actions or talk are instantly uncomfortable when the light gets close! Does Dustin love God? Does light emanate from him? Darkness fears that!

Do not be saddened when darkness attacks you. Be honored! You are doing something right. When you are in the darkness, get in the light. The darkness has to flee!

I learned in the crawl space that I depended on my flashlight. There were bugs down there! And who knows what else there was? That light kept fear away. But that light needed power.

Genieva Rice was one of the only people who knew about my crawl space before I got married. She was my amazing, God-loving grandma. I remember the night I told her about it. I must have been just barely six years old.

My grandma knew things were hard, and she longed to help however she could. What she did was provide for the needs I had in the crawl space. One of my needs were batteries. Big, D-cell batteries. The light took two, and they were the biggest batteries I had ever seen! She always gave me two at a time and would have me sneak them into the pocket of my jacket.

To keep the light bright in our lives, we need to recharge our battery at times! We have to connect to a power source.

Reading God's word and spending time in worship and prayer are great ways to keep your light bright.

Matthew 5:16 says this:

Let your light shine before others, that they may see your good deeds and glorify your Father in heaven.

When you give your life over to the tangible God, the Refuge, He gives you a job—to be a light. We live in a very dark world! Be a light in someone's darkness! Just another valuable lesson I learned from my crawl space.

Chapter 4: *Find it before you need it*

We moved into our new house when I was six years old. In fact, it was not very long before Mount St. Helens blew. I remember how much I loved our house. No one had ever lived there before. It was brand new and it was all ours! I honestly don't remember very much from before I was six, but I remember that pretty new house. I remember my mom showing me my new bedroom and I remember putting up my new bed. I remember being excited to unpack my picture books and my Strawberry Shortcake dolls. As I explored my new room over the next few weeks, I remember seeing the line in the carpet. I remember feeling the edge of the line that revealed a cut. I pried it open to expose a shallow, dirt-floored room. I explored it and thought it was so cool! I visited it often. It was oddly shaped and had some cobwebs, but that was not enough to deter me. I had an adventure in my own room.

I was seven before I used it as a hiding place for the first time, and nearly eight by the time it became just a cool hideout again.

The night I thought to use it as a panic room of sorts was a terrifying one. I still remember the smell of alcohol on my father's breath when he returned home from work. I had no flashlight yet. I would dig that out of our camping supplies the very next day after my father left for work. I remember thinking, it is *there* I could hide. I was afraid my absence would be noticed, but the Lord was on my side. And if my mother saw I was gone, she didn't mention it to anyone. But from inside the crawl space, I could hear my father's footsteps in my room during his episode and then I heard him leave. At some point that night I slipped back out of the hole and crawled back into my bed with a peaceful feeling that all was well.

What is the connection here? What is the lesson learned? Before the trouble comes, know where it is that you can run. Whether the place of safety you need is psychological or physical, know where to run. Get acquainted with your hiding place.

Psalm 32:7 says,

> *You are my hiding place;*
>
> *You will protect me from trouble*
>
> *And surround me with songs of deliverance.*

I remember an old song, one that still touches my heart. It makes me go back to times when I needed trust more than anything.

It said,

> *You are my hiding place*
>
> *You always fill my heart with songs*
>
> *Of deliverance, whenever I am afraid*
>
> *I will trust in you*
>
> *I will trust in you*
>
> *I will trust in you*
>
> *Whenever I am afraid*

I remember singing this song. I remember my grandmother having it on an old Maranatha CD. I think I was seven or eight when it came out. I remember singing this song in my head towards the end of my parents' marriage. It was my very own hiding place.

Is Jesus your hiding place? In the mist of your hard times, does He fill your heart with a song of deliverance? When you are afraid, do you know where to run? And in times of severe trouble, can you depend on Him to show you where your help comes from? As much as we may only want our troubles to be between us and God, He may at times shed light in a situation and bring us someone or something to help us. It is simply amazing what God can do when we come to Him.

One more thing to remember is this: we get to come to Him broken. I at no point in my life could have fixed myself. That was only to be done by the One who made me. All I had to do was seek refuge. Then God went on with the task of putting the pieces back together. I know there were some pieces that were lost deep inside me. Those pieces had to be dug out before they could be put back together. It took time. Have patience still, for God is not finished with me yet. What you get when you find Jesus as your refuge is *hope*. Without hope I have nothing. This is the lesson that I learned the hard way!

Chapter 5: *Unreachable*

The worst memory I have from grade school is one that I almost never talk about or share. It is one that to me seems like a "just get over it" kind of deal. But yet, this one moment in time is hands down one of the worst recollections for me. I still have this memory pop into my head at times and it raises chills all over me and makes me feel ill! Okay I need to just spit it out, because it has only been recently that I have figured out the reason it affects me so deeply.

I was in third grade and our school was having its annual hoedown. For this event, each family had to buy tickets in advance to hold its place for a meal. I hated any kind of after-school event and, frankly, I think my sister did as well.

As a way to drown out his pain, fear, and anger, my father drank. A lot! When he came home from work, you never knew what you were going to get—melancholy, sober, quiet Dad; loud, happy-go-lucky, drunk Dad; or *mean* drunk Dad. It would depend on how much and what he had to drink after work. He was a happy beer drunk but with hard liquor, he didn't fare as well.

On hoedown night he was the happy-go-lucky, loud, overly fun Dad and he was ready to paint the town. He saw a flyer for the hoedown sitting on the table.

I wanted to run and hide to make it all go away. I believe that this is the time where, if I had had the capacity for suicidal thoughts, they would have come.

I remember his voice saying, "Let's go, it's a hoedown!" He said it over and over again in a western drawl. I tried to convince him that you had to pre-order the tickets so we wouldn't be able to go. But I had to be careful, for one word taken as disrespect would lead to consequences that did not fit the crime.

With a look to my sister, we both got in the car, heads hung low.

My mother was at work. There was no hope of her talking him down.

Upon arriving at the event, I was already fighting back the tears. I was angry at my father and I was angry at God. I wanted my crawl space, my refuge. I had prayed. I had hoped. Yet here I was walking into my own personal mental hell! To make it worse, all of the kids who already thought I was a loser were there to share in my moment.

My father strode into my school and went to the sign-in table where he explained in a slur how his kids never told him about the hoedown and he wanted to come. The event was already 30 mins in full swing. One of the teachers helped us find a table and got us food. I sat down and tried to eat a piece of corn on the cob, but I knew somehow I was never going back to school, not ever again. Humility might be a hard thing for an eight-year-old to grasp, but humiliation is another story. I was mortified, humiliated, and hurt. Jesus did not rescue me and I was done with Him!

Crawl space unreachable. Mission failure! Where was God? He said He would be there. I felt so alone.

What do you do when you feel let down by God? When you are humiliated, hurt, confused, lost, and flat out angry?

When has God seemed unreachable to you? I know it seems childish, but that was a big one for me!

Well, I *was* a child. And I grew up, finished school, and good for me, I got to run away to college and never return. But what would my situation be when the pain of life became bigger?

The loss of a child, the betrayal of a spouse, the poor decisions of kids that will affect the rest of their lives—what then? When your spouse is diagnosed with cancer, your house burns to the ground, or your job of 25 years is terminated . . . these, these things are real. And they hurt.

The lesson I learned in this situation I did not grasp until I was in college. And that is this: God did not promise me a perfect life if I chose to follow Him; He promised me an *everlasting* life. And God did not promise me He would keep all the bad away from me; He promised me He would help me *through* it! And He has.

I have been blessed with the most amazing husband on earth. He is my rock. I often joke with him and others that he rescued me like a knight on a white horse, that he saved the princess in despair. In fact, that is kind of what happened! You see, God gave me a partner to go through the hard stuff with. He gave me a man who made me believe that, even with all of my scars and baggage, I was worthy of love from someone besides my Creator.

I have also been blessed with the best of friends and an amazing support group. I don't know how I managed to get hooked up with the best people. God has a way of knowing just whom I need and when!

The thing is, God is looking out for me. He always wants what's best for me. But God doesn't reach down to the people to whom He gave free will and control them like puppets. Therefore, my wrongdoings as well as the wrongdoings of others create problems! Life is life— sometimes bad things just happen. There are hurt, sickness, disloyalty, and death in this world.

The hope in it all is that God did not come to earth and die on a cross for us for nothing. He doesn't condemn us to an awful life with no hope. He has prepared a place for us to one day go and spend eternity with Him and it is simply gonna rock!

At times God may seem far away, yet he never leaves me. There are times in life where we are raw and exposed and we can't find a place to take refuge. Yet we know that God is there, like a bomb shelter He covers us. Not to mention all we have to do is look around and we can see God's hand, sending us people, care, and protection on a regular basis.

Perfection is unreachable, but God is very reachable! We lose sight of the end goal, but eternal life is promised to me! And when things are the darkest I know I can trust God to hold me. God is not unreachable.

Chapter 6: *The best things come to those who wait*

Have you ever wanted something so badly that you devoted everything to hoping for it? As much as the following words could make me sound like a bit of a jerk, I will share them anyway.

Throwing caution to the wind, I tell you this. From age five to age eight, my biggest hope, my deepest longing, and my most persistent prayer was this: "Lord Jesus, please take my scary daddy away." My father's PTSD made him scary and unpredictable.

I would sit in the crawl space or in my bedroom and I would pray this prayer. Over and over. Day after day. The prayer didn't change. I longed for change. I wanted to live without fear.

Little did I know that in the very next room, my sweet sister was praying a very different prayer. Her prayer was more like this: "Dear God, please don't let my Daddy leave. Please help Mommy and Daddy stop fighting. Please help my Daddy. Please fix him, Lord." Unbeknownst to either of us, my sister and I were both about to have the answers to our prayers.

In July of 1983, I got on a plane with my sister and my stuffed cat Heathcliff and we headed to Alaska. I was scared to death of flying and I clung to my cat on our Horizon Airlines flight. We had a plane change in Juneau where we would get on a small Cessna headed to

Haines. Somewhere in the switch from plane one to plane two, I lost Heathcliff. He would never be seen again. I cried from Juneau to Haines and all the way to my grandparents' house. I had lost my comfort. We stayed in Alaska for a month. Losing my cat friend on the way was a very vivid foreshadowing of how the month would play out! There were some good parts, though – I got to know my Alaskan grandparents, I made new friends, went fishing with my Grandpa Ray, and learned to ride horses.

Late August we returned home and were picked up not by two, but by one parent. When we arrived at the house, our father's stuff had all been removed. In his place was a small dog named Beau Beau. It was a birthday/goodbye gift from my father to my sister.

That hot August day I realized that God had finally answered my prayer! My father was gone! I also realized my mother and sister were broken because my prayers were answered. The next two years were complete and total hell for me. There was still so much fear. Due to another life changing set of events, there were lawyers and court appearances! And then there was the fear that my father would come to our school and try to take us! I began to wonder if I had asked for the wrong thing with my prayers.

Over the years, things did get better. There were some really great times, like camping trips, family meetings, and lobster dinners at the Cattle Company. My mom even received a gift certificate award from work. I grew somewhat comfortable.

My mother, however, was sad and lonely. Finances were very tight and my sister and I worked hard to keep meals made and the house picked up. All the while my sister kept praying that God would save my dad, and that he would come home.

During my seventh grade year my father tried to end his life. The PTSD had caught up to him! The mental anguish of Vietnam overwhelmed him. Alcohol had become his only friend and he decided life was too hard. He jumped from a moving vehicle. Dove out of the car, head on. He did not succeed at this death attempt.

My father nearly died, but the doctors were able to save him. And thus began the spiral into my father's personal hell. From the hospital my father went to a mental health facility. From there he lived in a Portland homeless hostel/hotel. From there it just got worse.

I remember very well the day the courts gave my father the guilty verdict after he had been picked up on yet another DUI. I thought, good for him. Serves him right. Yet while I was drowning in my bitterness, one state over at a college in Washington State, my sister was still praying for my father's salvation.

As I hated – she prayed. As I was bitter, her tenderhearted spirit thrived. While I wished for condemnation, she wished for change. I could write a whole other book on the lesson I learned from my sister! By my eleventh grade year my father was released from the Oregon State Penitentiary. And I didn't care a bit what happened to him next. But then, I went to summer camp.

When Stan Russell got up and spoke about the anger and hurt we pack around with us, he dared us to forgive. Stan challenged us to trust God to make things better. As I walked up to that old wooden alter at Camp Davidson, I started to weep! Pastor Rich Wood came and prayed with me as well. With Pastor Stan on one side and Pastor Rich on the other, I literally wailed to the Lord. I remember being in physical pain as I allowed all the years of hurt to rise to the surface and released them to the Almighty God. I sat at that alter until after midnight and bless their hearts, the pastors prayed with me for as long as it took. They will always have a very special place in my heart.

I was not the same when I came home from that camp. I had been changed and I was determined that my senior year would not be spent the way my previous years were.

You see, while in prison my father gave his heart to Jesus. And at camp, I accepted that even my dad deserved forgiveness. That was a big acceptance for me!

My sister showed me that the best things come to those who wait upon the Lord.

Those who wait upon the Lord shall renew their strength. They will mount up with wings like eagles, run and not grow weary. God allowed Roxanne to be constantly renewed as she continued to pray for God's best.

The summer following my twelfth grade year, my parents remarried. God had a plan. He knew the bigger picture. It was not all about me! It was about a family, one that he would begin to restore piece by piece. I would begin to see peace and renewal in the next generation because of this healing.

My selfish plans of wanting my father to go away collided with God's perfect plan for my father to find Him. My sister's broken heart, caused by coming home to a house my father had abandoned, was renewed when my father returned, a new creation in Christ. Thanks to prison ministry, my father found the Lord and his hope was renewed in that seemingly Godforsaken place.

Sometimes we simply cannot see what God is doing and waiting for Him to work can be painful. But, as we wait, as we watch Him do His good things, we begin to see it is true.

The best things truly come to those who wait.

Chapter 7: *Flawless grace*

A while ago a song was released by Mercy Me, titled "Flawless." The first time I heard it I was drawn to it. Each time after that, I was mesmerized by it. The song reminds me that it is the flawless grace of God that has made me the woman that I am today.

You see, I should never have fared as well as I have. I live under the strong understanding that, but for the grace of God, there go I.

I love the line in the song that says this:

> *Then like a hero who takes the stage when*
>
> *We're on the edge of our seats saying it's too late*
>
> *Well let me introduce you to amazing grace*

Those words are a masterpiece!

When we feel too broken or too used; when life seems too hard for us to go on; when we think we are too bad to be forgiven; that is when Jesus, the superhero, steps in. He reminds us that He already came and sacrificed His life so that we could be recipients of amazing grace.

I was only six the first time Charles approached me. I was just a baby. His intentions with me were far less than pure.

I had seen him before. Charles was not a stranger. He was the best friend of our next door neighbor.

His touch was very harmless the first time. But it wasn't long before one day I was lured behind a tall wooden privacy fence at the end of my road. That day would change me forever.

As a kid, I always went to the end of the road and threw a basketball at the hoop constructed there.

One day I went to the end of the road, as usual. I was wearing a pink and brown bathing suit. It was about 80 degrees outside. I had been playing in the sprinkler at my friend Gwen's house and she had to go in. He did things to me that day. Things a thirty-something-year-old man should never do to a six-year-old baby.

I wanted to tell. I wanted to make it go away. I wanted to suddenly have a take-back, a do-over. That day it was not my father, but an awful criminal named Charles, who sent me to that crawl space.

As I sat there with my flashlight, I shook. I was still in my swim suit. It was chilly in the underground dugout. It was there I decided I would never tell a soul what he had done.

Fear cripples us. Shock lowers our ability to think clearly and time allows us to block it all out—to try to forget. But we never forget. Little girls don't forget the threats spoken to them in scary places when they are all alone. Little girls don't forget inappropriate touches from scary men they feel powerless against.

It would be three years before I spoke a word of it to anyone. Then one day I went to my neighbor's house. I was in the third grade and her daughters were in second and fourth. That day I went over to see if the girls could play, but they had gone somewhere with their dad. Carlene, the lady of the house, asked me if I would like to sit and have a glass of lemonade with her. I said sure. As we sat in her side yard at a small table, she asked me a question. She said, "Amy, has anyone ever done anything inappropriate to you?" I said no. I was getting nervous. She said, "I mean like, touch you in a way they shouldn't?" I said "I need to go now!" Carlene said these words next: "Did he tell you he would hurt you if you told?" Carlene took my hand and the tears began to fall. "No," I said, "not me. He said he would kill my family. He would hurt my sister. If I did what he wanted it would be okay." Carlene explained to me how he was lying so he could get away with something that he should not have done. And that reminded me of how strong my dad was. I begged Carlene not to tell my parents. She said, okay, if I told them, she wouldn't. So I worked up the courage and I told my mom.

Carlene later told my mother that she had been abused herself. She said that she saw the signs in me. And she simply could not stay silent.

That year any bit of self-esteem I had was crushed to bits as I sat on the stand in that court room. If you can make an eight-year-old look like a whore, then that is what Charles's lawyer did to me. Charles had a good lawyer. My neighbor, who was my father's best friend, was on Charles's side, and talked about how I often made things up and acted provocatively, waltzing around the neighborhood in my polka dot bikini. I was only six when it happened, I was honest, and I had no idea what provocative meant. I died a little inside during those months. I knew I was dirty and unlovable. I was yucky and I would feel that and worse for many years to come.

The courts said it didn't happen. I lost the court case. I was labeled a liar. I believed there were moments when even my parents questioned my honesty. My lawyer told me I had waited too long to tell and there were holes in my story.

I was broken, but not beyond repair. I felt dirty, stained, and labeled. But I was not out of the reach of God's grace.

Just a few years later, it was discovered that there were other children in the neighborhood who were also abused by the criminal. Included on that list of kids were the sons of my neighbor—the same man who had defended his friend at my trial and called me things that left a mess of scars, my father's own friend.

One day I came home from school, got off the bus, and was greeted by my mother. I was a latchkey kid. My mother never came to the bus stop. And today she had puffy eyes. I think I was in the sixth grade. My mom took me and the other neighborhood kids out to ice cream. It was very strange because the street I lived on was full of cops and emergency vehicles. I found out that evening that my neighbor's dad had killed himself in their garage. The guilt overtook him. I felt horrible. I wished then that I had never said a word about Charles.

I went on to junior high and started feeling exceedingly out of control of my life. I developed eating disorders and by high school, began to sneak drinks with my non-school friends. I had to hide. I could not be Amy the Broken. I was so lost.

As a high schooler, with my dad in prison and the whole world knowing about it, I felt like a big time screw up. You don't get much more broken than that!

You see, grace is not only for those of us who come in a pretty package. It is not just for the ones who have it all together, or those who seem to have no problems! You see, the Bible says that none of us has it all together. For *all* have sinned and fallen short of God's best. Grace is for the sinner. God's renewal is for the broken. His cleansing is for the ones who feel dirty. God sees none of us as damaged goods. He sees, instead, His creation. Children of God. Created in His image. *Imago dei.*

I came to Jesus hurting and broken. He fixed me up. He planted my feet back on solid ground! Jesus is my super hero. Jesus is my everything—my amazing grace, my flawless. The cross was enough for me.

Flawless grace. I need it every day. His amazing, flawless grace covers my sin, my shame, my guilt, the wrongs done against me, and my every pain. Let His flawless grace be enough for you.

Chapter 8: *To have a friend, be a friend*

There is no part of junior high that is easy. We are all dying to make friends! This was one of my hardest years ever. I had about three friends while in the seventh grade, and they were all about as different as night and day. I had a "bestie." I had another friend who was a model – she was drop dead gorgeous and had a killer figure. Thinking back, my guess is that she was about as messed up as me. But she was always there to hang out with, and I remember feeling shocked that someone as pretty as Elle would ever want to hang with me. And, then, I had the goofy guy BFF whom I loved because he made me laugh.

My life had been challenge after challenge. At this point, I'd never told a soul about how challenging it had been, until one night at a sleepover I told bits of my story to my best friend.

It was a week or so later that God brought into my life my forever friend Natalie. We met at school. She was the new girl, straight out of Catholic girls' school, and she barely knew a soul. The day we met was the beginning of a friendship forged by God.

I remember Natalie coming up to me, saying, "I think you need to know what that girl told me about you." My so-called bestie was no friend at all. She had stabbed me in the back and shared my deep, dark secrets with several other people.

I was stunned and hurt. I needed a friend I could trust, and so did Nat. With every one of life's ups and downs, we have stuck together. Through our accomplishments and through our times that were lower than low, Natalie and I stuck together. To this day she is my bestie for life, the one who didn't abandon me—ever.

It is hard to know whom to trust! Sometimes life can get pretty lonely when we feel like we have no one to share with! But Jesus is always trustworthy. He will never let me down!

Jesus is a friend who sticks closer than a brother. He loves me with a love that has no limits. I know I will never be alone.

Regardless, we all long for physical friends. I believe God has them for us when we need them. God puts them in our lives for reasons we may never see.

Over the years I have felt this challenge. Be a friend others can trust. Be the friend you want others to be to you!

Over the years my pool of friends has grown. I have some absolutely awesome friends. I thank God for all of them. I want to make sure I am always the friend to them that I hope for them to be to me!

Yet I am broken – this is what I am. Sometimes I am a jerk. I do or say the wrong things. I lose my temper at times. And although sometimes I try not to be, I do get judgmental about things or people. I've done so much wrong, yet Jesus has forgiven me. But what about Charles and my dad? Did they deserve God's amazing grace as well?

I would love to say that I accepted the need to forgive Charles as easily as I accepted the need to forgive my dad at the altar at summer camp. Unfortunately, I let my disgust, brokenness, and hatred for Charles stick with me a lot longer than I should have. I was married, with children, and active in ministry before I let go of that pain.

The broken place I lived in stunted my growth. It lowered my self-image and clouded my life view. I let his sin and perversion mold me. There was a point in my adult life where I had to say, "enough is enough. I will not let this man ruin me!" Isn't it funny how we feel bad because of the sins of others? The day I confessed my hatred to God was the day I finally felt freedom from it. That day I discovered that forgiveness of another person does not mean we condone their behavior, accept responsibility for their bad choices, or even let up our guard of self-protection. Forgiveness meant that I was finally going to let it go. It was time to turn his perversion over to God. I was not the one who was going to hold him accountable for his wrongs. I needed to let those wrongs stay in the past, allowing God the Healer to be faithful, to continue the good work that He had begun in me! At times I needed the help of friends, and often the help of my husband to navigate through all the muck I swam in. With help from the friends God had placed in my life, and the mercy God gave me in each situation, I was able to forgive.

Forgiveness is freedom. It is only in forgiveness that we can be free from the chains that bind us to sadness, self-pity, and death! It was time for me to forgive and be free to live again! There were some amazing people that needed my best from me! I needed to be the best friend and mom that I could be, and that meant I had to let go of pain so I could forgive. Friends are a gift. But to have one, you must also be one.

Chapter 9: *What doesn't kill you makes you stronger*

I didn't understand her inner struggle. It was not until many years later that I could feel her pain. I didn't agree with her choice. I could not grasp what I saw as her weakness or her desperation.

I would get into the car because of my mother's enticement to let me drive. We would head out—my mother, occasionally my sister, and I—and begin the trek to the Oregon State Penitentiary. It was about an hour's drive. On the way there we would talk. On the way home there was usually considerably less chit chat.

I hated going. I hated the prison. I was unsure how I felt about the man we were going to see. But it was not my father that made it hard to visit the prison. There was another reason.

You had to be mentally and physically prepared to walk into that place. The visitation room was a big tan concrete box. I would get through the metal detectors, show my ID, go through the hoops, and walk through the doors and into the small room; then a guard would open the second door and I would begin to scan. I knew he was here. My father had told me. I knew he could have a visitor anytime I was there. My father had told me that he wanted to kill him. This actually endeared my father to me, just a bit.

I remember the first time he was there. He sat a few tables away. And I was drawn to peek at him like a weird bee-to-pollen scenario. When I looked at him he caught my eyes. He smiled at me and mouthed the words, *I will get you*. He was just trying to get to me—trying to scare me. And it worked.

I asked my mom if we could leave. She said, no, we just got here. She told me to just ignore him. How do you ignore the tiger in the room? It was not fair to ruin my mother and sister's visit, and we only had a short time. I could make it. I did see compassion in my father's eyes for one of the first times ever. I know he hated himself for being there so that we all had to be.

I sat in that room feeling wounded. I was face to face with both of the men I longed to hide from.

I truly felt vulnerable that day. I sat wanting someone to save me. I was drowning and no one came to my rescue. I was angry at my mother. I was angry at the world. I didn't understand the importance of the visits to my dad in prison or the importance they had to my mother. Now I can see.

It took a while for me to get over this one. I was a grown adult before I began to find peace from the trauma of that day. You see, at some point it hit me—my parents had a love story. To me it was warped and messed up. It was broken and chipped in places. But the fact was, she *loved* him. My mother wanted to give him a piece of normalcy, an hour of reprieve from the hell that prison was. I was being a cement block and my tantrum was keeping that wish of hers from coming to pass.

I survived. I am here to tell you that on the other side of it all, I am alive and I am stronger. It was hard and I was bruised, but I am not broken.

Matthew 12:20 says this:

A bruised reed he will not break and a smoldering wick

he will not snuff out.

It was several years later that Natalie Grant wrote a song entitled "The Real Me" that was instrumental in bringing me to the place where I found me again.

Foolish heart looks like we're here again

Same old game of plastic smile

Don't let anybody in

Hiding my heartache, will this glass house break

How much will they take before I'm empty

Do I let it show, does anybody know?

But you see the real me

Hiding in my skin, broken from within

Unveil me completely

I'm loosening my grasp

There's no need to mask my frailty

Cause you see the real me

Painted on, life is behind a mask

Self-inflicted circus clown

I'm tired of the song and dance

Living a charade, always on parade

What a mess I've made of my existence

But you love me even now

And still I see somehow

But you see the real me

Hiding in my skin, broken from within

Unveil me completely

I'm loosening my grasp

There's no need to mask my frailty

Cause you see the real me

Wonderful, beautiful is what you see

When you look at me

You're turning the tattered fabric of my life into

A perfect tapestry

I just wanna be me

But you see the real me

Hiding in my skin, broken from within

Unveil me completely

I'm loosening my grasp

There's no need to mask my frailty

Cause you see the real me

And you love me just as I am

Wonderful, beautiful is what you see

When you look at me

I no longer had to hide behind the mask that hid my tears. I realized the God truly saw the real me, the person I was hiding inside me—the me that was broken. I began to grasp the life changing power of Jesus Christ. I began to realize that God could take the broken pieces and not just put them back together, but make me stronger than ever. I am a new creation in Christ. The old has passed and the new has come.

What is it in your life that is causing you slow, internal death? Let me tell you this: Jesus knows, Jesus cares, and if you can come to a place of surrender to Him, Jesus will carry it for you. We are given the opportunity to trade our sorrows for the joy of the Lord.

The day I realized that what my mother did that day was not about a lack of tolerance for me, but a deep love and compassion for my father. I found a piece of forgiveness that I never thought I could give. And I learned without a shadow of a doubt, that what does not kill us makes us stronger.

Chapter 10: *Mourning is allowed*

I am sure I would have been a daddy's girl. I just never had the opportunity until the crucial moment of bonding had passed me by.

I am sure my life would have been different if there had been no Vietnam War.

I am sure that if I had never met Charles, I would have had a higher self-worth as a young person.

I am sure that if I didn't have learning disabilities, I would have thought I was smarter.

I am sure if I had felt beautiful as a young girl, I would not long to think that someone believes I am today.

Loss! Deprivation! Death of our self-worth. Theft of our childhood. These are things that need to be mourned. I was in my thirties when I began mourning.

Great is thy faithfulness, great is thy faithfulness!

Morning by morning new mercies I see.

All I have needed thy hand hath provided.

Great is the faithfulness Lord unto me.

As I poured tears over the loss of my innocence; as I grieved the fact that any semblance of having a "normal" daddy was stolen from me; and as I gave up the longing to fix it all—I found healing.

God's mercies were new every morning. I literally traded my sorrows for His joy. Mourning brought new life.

I may never have gotten to be the daddy's girl I longed to be, but as I watch my beautiful baby girl build a wonderful relationship with *her* amazing daddy, I am blessed. I experience it second hand.

I may have lost the innocence of childhood, but I rejoice in the privilege of raising my own three beautiful kids. Watching them be kids I one of my greatest joys.

I may have missed out on feeling safe and beautiful, but my own children will not feel the same. I will indeed make sure that is the case.

I may have felt alone in my fears and my pain, but the students I minister to will always know I am here for them. I became a counselor and a children's pastor for a reason.

God has restored to me what was lost. And I will be there for others to let the Lord use my story for good. That is what God does: He turns ashes to beauty. We mourn our losses and His love restores.

Chapter 11: *Saying I'm sorry*

The white flag was raised. My father was in a place of surrender. He wanted to be my friend and he longed to be my father.

After he was released from prison, my father was a very different man. He began to seek after me. He would apologize often and he was filled with a guilt that was hard for him to let go of.

It was the summer after my senior year that my parents remarried and they finally seemed happy. I decided after camp that forgiveness for my father was actually not as hard as I had thought it would be. The war had changed my dad. He used to be fun-loving, witty, and funny. I had never known him to be such, but had heard the stories. Enough to get a glimpse of the man he used to be. I now realize how much my son Derek is in some ways like him in personality. When I look at it that way, I can imagine my sweet, loving, funny, lighthearted Derek in place of my dad. Then, my dad becomes a young man from a troubled home. Throw in a war that had not only scared a few men, but rather an entire nation.

My father did not have a chance. He was strong. He was built like a ninja, I always thought. But inside he was just a broken boy. I am not sure exactly when I started to hear the "I am sorry's" for what they were—sincere. But when I did, I found yet more freedom.

There is freedom in saying you are sorry, freedom in owning that we did wrong. And there is also freedom in accepting the apology of someone else.

For years in the ministry, I practiced a certain philosophy of never letting others see you make a mistake. Hide your wrongs from the world, fix them and put them away. This is *not* a philosophy I support. For if the leaders cannot own their mistakes, how can we expect anyone else to?

I adopted a new principle in life and with my own kids. They know that their mom screws up constantly. I've tried to teach them this lesson that I learned from my post-crawl-space father. I no longer had to hide from my dad. In his brokenness he has become one of the most sorry and humble men I know.

My children make mistakes, parents make mistakes, you will make mistakes, and so will I. Learn to say you're sorry and learn to give forgiveness. If you can do these two things, you are heading in the right direction toward becoming humble and kind.

By allowing yourself to forgive and be forgiven, you accept the freedom that comes with it. Be quick to accept your mistakes and be quick to say "I'm sorry." There is freedom found there.

Chapter 12: *Forgive yourself*

Not a day went by during my freshman year of college where my father, if I talked to him on the phone, would not say "I'm sorry" at least once. My father lived in serious torment, haunted by the wrongs that he had caused. There comes a time in everyone's life where we must, in order to let go of the past, forgive ourselves.

Forgiving others can be hard. Forgiving yourself seems impossible in comparison. But in order to truly be free from our mistakes and the pain that they bring, we have to learn how to forgive ourselves.

Years went by. Every phone conversation and every face-to-face interaction would start and end with an apology of some kind. Even though my family had forgiven my father, our forgiveness was hard for him to accept. I believe the reason for his lack of acceptance was the fact that my father had not forgiven himself.

I remember the trip to Oregon when I first noticed the changes in my father. My dad was aggravated and did not seem like his usual self. I had no idea what was the matter, but I knew something was wrong.

Months later we discovered that my dad had Alzheimer's. The initial diagnosis was very scary.

What would happen now? How would this man handle this debilitating disease? Little did we know that the memory loss that accompanied Alzheimer's would be my father's, and our, little gift from God.

My father has had some form of dementia for about 12 years now. It is no longer being called Alzheimer's, because in these 12 years there has been almost no mental decline. However, he has lost many of his memories of war, childhood, prison, and mine and my sister's childhoods.

My father could not figure out how to forgive himself. I believe that the Almighty God gave him an out. He took away the memories, and along with them, the guilt. The daily phrase "I'm sorry" also ceased to exist, and we were given the gift of having a fun-loving, zany, yet very forgetful father.

What have you done that seems unforgivable? Cast it upon the Lord. He will forgive you. And although it may take time, others will eventually forgive you as well. If they choose not to, that is their problem. They have to deal with those consequences. Give yourself the gift of forgiveness, and remember to give that gift to others as well.

Chapter 13: *The most debilitating disability in life is a bad attitude*

I can still see it, the pink rubber tennis ball hanging from the ceiling, the pen floating from side to side in front of my face. The five different pairs of glasses I hid in various places around my neighborhood.

I was diagnosed as dyslexic before dyslexia was cool. When I entered the third grade I still couldn't read, I really struggled in math, and I was very introverted and withdrawn. With all that had been going on, my life was a bit of a mess. At school I rarely spoke. If you know me in any capacity today, you might find that very hard to believe.

In the third grade I had the most amazing teacher. She helped me through so much! Her name was Mrs. Prentiss. Mrs. Prentiss told me I was smart. That was something I had not heard much, really. I had gotten through kindergarten by being a fabulous memorizer. Mrs. Prentiss saw right through that. I am not sure how it all came to pass, but somehow I ended up in an experimental new program to help kids with dyslexia and similar learning disabilities.

We took weekly trips to Pacific University. At PU, I was taught how to look at things in a different way. I learned to put the floating letters together in ways that made sense and how to logically decipher which way things should go. We turned my room into a virtual gymnasium where my eyes would follow balls hanging on the ceiling while I learned how to track with my eyes. By my second time through third grade, I was reading fairly well. Mrs. Prentiss got married and became Mrs. Scott. I was fortunate enough to have her for the third grade twice.

I remember my amazing teacher telling me that I was very smart to be catching on so quickly. She convinced me that I was not stupid. Both years of third grade were very hard. I was still teased a lot, and other kids called me stupid and retarded. But I loved going to school because Mrs. Prentiss was there. And most days after school, she tutored me. She helped me learned to read, asked me questions about how I was. She brought me candy treats and showed me the love I needed so badly. Mrs. Prentiss never treated me like I was broken.

When the pages of this book are in print, I will make sure she gets a copy. I will make sure she knows how much she inspired the life of a third grade girl.

The lesson I took from Mrs. Prentiss was this: attitude is everything. I can still hear her telling me, "Amy, they can only hurt you if you let them." "Amy, let the words of those kids roll off like water off a duck's back." "Amy, if you believe you can, you can! It is all in your attitude."

Now I tell my students this often. I have written curriculum revolving around these principles. I have spoken on the topic at leadership seminars. I believe that attitude is everything. You can change your circumstances by changing your outlook. And in my darkest times, I have pulled from the deepest depths to find an attitude that was glorifying to God.

I was able to overcome my learning disabilities, but it is hard to come out on top if you have a bad attitude. Obstacles can be hurdled and road blocks can be avoided. Bad attitudes simply compound the problems. What are the attitudes holding you back? Let them go like water off a ducks back! You hold the power to having a better day. Attitude is everything!

Chapter 14: *We are here to make a difference*

One day she realized that she was not born to hide away but to SHINE brightly! So she decided to stop listening to her fears and finally focus on what made her feel truly alive

-Anna Taylor

I have been asked before, if you could start it all again, if you could not have to go through all the things you went through, would you do it? If you could snap your fingers and change your fate, would you?

I have to say no! Trials in my life have built character in me. I am *so* far from perfect. I am still a big fat beautiful mess, but my experiences have helped make a difference in people's lives.

Many years ago I met a girl who was fighting with her self-worth. She was struggling with eating disorders and needed someone to just listen to her. I was able to be that person.

A few years ago I was blessed to love on some young ladies whose father had been sent to prison. They needed me!

Not long ago a young lady came to my office in tears. She wanted to end her life because of the abuse she was enduring. In the right timing, I was able to share my story and not only is she alive and kicking today, but she is safe serving Jesus.

I have had students who struggled with hatred and forgiveness. Couples who were on the verge of divorce and children who were struggling with school who just needed to be told they were smart so they could begin to believe it.

The job I have ended up in has led me to place after place where I have landed in the lives of broken people. Beautifully broken messes that, like a kaleidoscope of color, have displayed to me that I can make something beautiful with my own story.

I am here to make a difference. So are you!

We all have a story. We were not meant to hide it. This is merely a glimpse of mine. There is so much more. The things I share with others are allowed only when the time is right. It was my time to stop focusing on my fear and start believing for direction from the One who makes me feel alive!

What is your story? How can you use it? We all have a crawl space of some kind. What are the lessons you learned? I wish I could hear them all. Maybe one day I can hear some.

It is your turn to shine. Grow from your story; share your story. I hope you have been inspired by my lessons from the crawl space! Now it is time to find peace with your own story. Who knows which life is out there, just waiting for your story to be a catalyst for life change?

Chapter 15: *Be the one who cared*

Sometimes things would get really bad. My mother would signal my sister and I to sneak to the car. I can picture my mother running to the car and pulling away as fast as she could. It was like a scene from a movie.

When you need to flee but you cannot run to anyone you know for protection, where do you go?

I remember them. I remember what they did for us; however, I cannot remember their names.

We drove for quite a while. My sister held my hand in the back seat of the car. We arrived late. It was dark and quiet and my mom was crying. My mom didn't cry often.

The ladies took us in, the ones who worked at Portland's battered women's shelter. They gave us a room to sleep in where we could all stay together. They gave my sister and me each a bear. I hugged that bear tightly. The next day when we woke up, the nice ladies gave us fresh clothes to wear. They fed us and gave us each a toothbrush and a hair brush. It was still very scary, but these ladies we met were very nice.

I often in the weeks to follow had the thought: why did we ever leave those nice people? Why did we go back home? There were a few times when my sister and I stayed there and my mom left. I wondered, did she go to her job? She would have been safe there. She worked at a secure lab. There were security guards and badges. He couldn't get her there. Did she go see him to talk things out? To this day I do not know; I never had the nerve to ask. But after a couple days, we went back home and he would be nicer. But I wasn't fooled. I knew the mean daddy would come back. The alternative would be too good to be true.

After we got home, I put my secret bear in my crawl space while my dad was at work. The lady had said I could talk to him. Sometimes I did, but mostly I talked to Jesus. But I held my bear close.

I learned something very valuable from the ladies at the shelter. Sometimes people need to know that there is something different to hope for. Somewhere better to dream of, someone out there who cares.

I promised myself at a very young age that I would be that someone who cared.

Those women didn't know me. They didn't get anything for treating me with kindness. Yet they did. They treated me like they cared. They most certainly didn't have to.

There came a time in my ministry where God began to bring me young people who needed to know someone cared. Young people whose parents were in the midst of awful divorces, kids who had been abused, kids who struggled with eating disorders, and kids who had learning disabilities—God allowed me to see them all.

There was nothing special about me, yet I had the honor of being someone who cared; I was being an extension of Jesus to kids in need. In more recent years, I have been able to be there for some adults as well. And I am honored every time I hear that still small voice in my heart that says, it is time to use your story again. Even if at times I am a little scared.

Look around you. Who in your world simply needs to know someone cares? In whose life can you make a difference?

We all have gifts, talents, and stories. Yours can all be used to help show someone that they are cared about.

Are you a baker? Maybe your elderly neighbor doesn't get a lot of visitors. Maybe a batch of cookies would brighten his day.

Are you a mechanic? Maybe the single mom at church needs an oil change and just offering to do it may be the act of kindness that shows her there is hope.

You are the world's light—a city on a hill, glowing in the night for all to see. Don't hide your light! Let it shine for all; let your good deeds glow for all to see, so that they will praise your heavenly Father.

Matthew 5:14-16

The kindness we show others lets them know we care. When we care, we are a light. I will be someone who cares.

This little light of mine, I'm gonna let it shine.

Epilogue: *Be the one you needed as a child*

I remember the first time I heard that statement. As I thought more about those words, I came to the realization that I had been living my life according to that statement long before I ever heard it.

I had some pretty amazing people in my life as a teenager. I owe so much thanks to both my youth pastors. Thanks Pastor Andy Smith, for seeing me through some tough times of insecurity as a junior-higher and young high-schooler. I owe another debt of gratitude to Pastor Roy Banker for reaching out to a lost junior in high school. He plugged me in at youth group and in adult services. He helped me find Jesus in a way I never had before. Roy and his wife gave me the positive attention and support I needed. I would not be the woman I am today without those Godly men.

I also had a mom who loved me very much. I was difficult to handle. I was so spirited and I know I was a handful. My mother knew that sometimes in life, the best support you can give your children is to let them go to the people God brings into their lives. I know now, after having my own children, how very hard that would be. Thanks Mom, for loving me enough to let me run, and for letting me leave our church. You only cared that I went to serve God somewhere.

So many men and women came in and out of my life. Teachers like Bernie Kuen, who helped me find my voice; and Lester Bean, the Hilhi librarian who spent hours helping me research Vietnam and the effects of PTSD, while listening to the endless chatter of a high school girl who was hurting.

Thank you Natalie, my high school best friend. I could have never made it through school without you. In a time when I so desperately needed a friend, God gave me you! You will never know how much you mean to me.

Roxanne, my amazing sister, you are a light in my life and I love you to the moon and back. Thanks for always being there for me!

Even as I have gotten older, the gifts of wonderful people never stop. I am surrounded by wonderful friends and family everywhere.

I have awesome kids, fantastic in-laws, and a wonderful ministry team.

I have the most amazing husband. God knew exactly what I needed when He put you into my life. Your gentle spirit and kind nature are a true gift to me. I love you so much.

Now I look at where I am, right here in the midst of life. I look at the trials I have faced. I also now look at the blessings I have and the love that fills my life, and I know that I am truly blessed. I consider it joy that I lived the life I have. I am thankful that, when I needed it most, I found my crawl space.

Lessons from the Crawl Space: Study Guide

Use the following pages as a guide to check on your own spiritual health. I hope you as the reader can go through the guide either alone or with a small group of trustworthy friends.

Happy studying.

Study Guide Chapter 1: Tangible
Psalm 27:5:

For in the day of trouble He will conceal me in His tabernacle; In the secret place of His tent He will hide me; He will lift me up on a rock.

We all have that place we go to when life becomes unbearable. Each of us has a place we run to when the going gets tough. For some of us, the place is tangible; for others, it is a place we go within the confines of our own mind. Having a getaway is very important. This chapter is a little extreme in its reasons for the need to hide. Yet, in life it seems we weekly, even daily have a need for a getaway. Without a place to go to slow down for a moment, to decompress, we become trapped.

Whether you are in a place of physical or emotional distress, or you are simply overwhelmed with life, a refuge is a must for you.

1. Where do you go when you are afraid? Is it a tangible place you run away to, or is it a place in your mind that offers mental refuge?

2. Where do you think the Lord wants us to run when life becomes too much for us?

We all need a Savior and a light in our darkness.

Psalms 27:1 says,

The Lord is my light and my salvation

Whom do you turn to when things get dark?

3. Are there times when you find it easy to trust in God? Are there times when you find it hard to trust in God? What have you learned about God after the hard times?

4. Have you ever feared that God will not protect you?

5. What does God's protection look like to you?

Psalm 46:1 says,

> *God is our refuge and strength, A very present help in trouble.*

6. What are you facing presently that you need refuge from, and are you ready to trust that the Lord can bring you safely on the other side of these struggles?

7. When your friends are in the dark, where do you lead them?

8. Once you find comfort in knowing that the Lord will bring you through to the other side of your trouble, do you think it is your responsibility to help your friends find where their comfort and refuge come from?

9. Do the following words apply to you? If so, how?

I will be a *listener*

I will be a *help*

I will *give*

I will be *present*

I will pay *attention*

I will be a *friend*

I will be a *bright spot* in someone's darkness

I will *sacrifice* my own time when I see a need

I will *let God use my story*

Look at this list. What areas describe you?

God has called you to make a difference in the lives of the people we come into contact with.

Let's remember, no matter what we are facing, God is the answer and God is our hope.

Study Guide Chapter 2: Quickly and quietly

In a world of noise, media, and distractions, it is very easy to get caught up in the fast and noisy of it all. Fast and noisy can be attractive.

1. In our walk with Jesus, what is the importance of "quickly and quietly"?

2. What are the things that distract you in your daily walk with the Lord?

3. What do you do to slow down and take time to clear your mind to refocus your mind on Christ?

Some distractions we face in life are simply normal: social media, family distractions, obligations, and such. These are life. It is important to make sure that in the midst of life, we still make time for God. Keeping God in the forefront of our doings can help our decision making.

Other distractions in life are not so normal. These distractions may cause us to exclude God from some areas of our lives altogether, things like what we are watching on television, what books we are reading, what we are looking at on the internet, and simply what we are doing or thinking about when we think no one is watching. Quickly running in the opposite direction from sinful temptation and quietly seeking refuge in the Lord has to be a part of daily life.

4. Are there tempting distractions in your life that are keeping your walk with God from reaching its greatest potential? What are these areas of weakness for you?

5. What are you doing to guard your heart from the sinful distractions of life that only lead to self-destruction?

6. What safety nets or accountabilities have you put in place to keep your eyes, ears, mouths, and hands from wandering into directions they should not go?

Oh, be careful little eyes what you see. Oh, be careful little ears what you hear. Oh, be careful little mouth what you say. Oh, be careful little feet where you go!

The Lord will fight for you, you only have to be silent

Exodus14:14

I find that when I can slow down and quietly put Christ in my mind, God takes over and it becomes much harder for me to keep my thoughts wrong. That is the Lord fighting for me.

Study Guide Chapter 3: Darkness cannot exist in light

It is interesting to look at darkness and light.

What happens when you put living things in the dark? They do not flourish. On the contrary, they die. Any plant that needs chlorophyll simply cannot be fed in the dark. Slowly they lose their color and begin to wither. This is very much how we as Christians respond to the literal "darkness" of evil. When we are surrounded with evil, what is good and life-giving inside of us is slowly killed.

Job 24:13, 15, & 17 says,

There are those who rebel against the light, who do not know its ways or stay in its paths... The eye of the adulterer watches for dusk; he thinks, 'No eye will see me,' and he keeps his face concealed... For all of them, deep darkness is their morning; they make friends with the terrors of darkness.

When we are sinning, we feel the need to hide what we are doing. When that sin comes into the light and we are forced to face it, we can then find renewal and help and we can begin to live again.

1. Why do you think we feel the need to hide when we are doing wrong?

2. Why do you think some find it acceptable to outwardly do evil things while others try to hide it?

John 3:19-21 states,

This is the judgment: that light has entered the world, and men have preferred darkness to light because their deeds were evil. Everybody who does wrong hates the light and keeps away from it, for fear his deeds may be exposed. But everybody who is living by the truth will come to the light to make it plain that all he has done has been done through God.

The dilemma is this: if we move into the light, it means that our sin is about to be exposed. We begin to count the costs. We know that God already knows, but now others will know as well. We suddenly work very hard to keep our wrongs hidden.

4. How is sin in the light freedom?

5. What happens when we keep our sin hidden for fear of exposure?

6. Where does sin in the dark eventually lead us?

7. When we openly confess our wrong doings and are forgiven, what are we given?

John 8:12:

I am the light of the world; anyone who follows me will not be walking in the dark; he will have the light of life.

Study Guide Chapter 4: Find it before you need it

Once the trouble is there is not the time to decide your safe place. The panic room is not built while the intruder is watching, waiting for you to get done before he attacks.

Before the trouble comes, know where it is that you can run. Whether the place of safety you need is psychological or physical, know where to run. Get acquainted with your hiding place.

Psalm 32:7 says,

You are my hiding place;

You will protect me from trouble

And surround me with songs of deliverance.

Time to think deep

1. Who are the people that God has put into your life that you can go to if you need help?

2. Who has God put into your life that you can talk about things with?

3. Where do you go when you need to get away and take time for yourself?

4. What does the word *safe* mean?

There are so many things in life that make us feel distance from God. Sometimes it is our own shortcomings, the sin that we get caught up in. Sometimes it is our state of mind, our depression, or our overwhelming hurt. Sometimes our feelings of peril, instability, or uncertainty in life come from a bitterness or anger inside of us.

Sin, depression, hurt, bitterness, and anger, although all different, all work a little bit the same. They eat us up from the inside out. If you notice a lump on your neck, and it seems to grow and grow, there needs to be a point where you no longer ignore it. Wounds left untreated fester and infect the rest of the body. Similarly, hurt people hurt others. You don't wait until you're dead to remove the cancer. In the same way, you do not wait for the unsafe things in your life to wound you before you run from them.

5. What things in your life need to be changed or removed so that you can feel safe?

Sometimes you have to travel a dark journey before you can see the light. Life often puts obstacles and troubles into our path. As much as we may want to believe that we can, we cannot just "get over it." I cringe sometimes when I hear people tell someone to just move on, just get over it. Healing takes time and wounds leave scars. Amputations leave phantom pains and sometimes revisiting the things that hurt us, with the intention of moving on, can help us to heal.

6. What is it in your life that you may need to revisit so that you can move on?

Study Guide Chapter 5: Unreachable

When the crawl space is unreachable,

And the mission is a failure!

Where is God?

What do you do when you feel left by God? When you are humiliated, hurt, confused, lost, and flat out angry?

Go to the Scriptures!

Joshua 1:9 (NIV)

Have I not commanded you?

Be strong and courageous.

Do not be afraid; do not be discouraged, for the Lord your God will be with you wherever you go."

Psalm 23 (NIV)

A psalm of David.

The Lord is my shepherd, I lack nothing.
He makes me lie down in green pastures,
he leads me beside quiet waters,
he refreshes my soul.
He guides me along the right paths
for his name's sake.
Even though I walk
through the darkest valley,
I will fear no evil,

for you are with me;
your rod and your staff,
they comfort me.

You prepare a table before me
in the presence of my enemies.
You anoint my head with oil;
my cup overflows.
Surely your goodness and love will follow me
all the days of my life,
and I will dwell in the house of the Lord
forever.

Matthew 28:20 (NIV)

And surely I am with you always, to the very end of the age.

Read the following scriptures and describe how each one gives you a hope that you are not alone.

Joshua 1:5

Zephaniah 3:17

Revelation 21:3

1. When has God seemed unreachable to you?

2. What have you experienced in life where God seemed quiet or distant?

The loss of a child, the betrayal of a spouse, the poor decisions of your kids that you are afraid will affect the rest of their lives, maybe a sick spouse, or the loss of a loved one. Maybe the loss of a house that has burnt to the ground, bankruptcy, or the loss of your job?

3. Think back to your times of trouble, then think of the previous scriptures. Were there any God moments in the struggles where you knew that God was, in fact, with you?

The lesson: God did not promise me a perfect life if I chose to follow Him; He promised me an *everlasting* life. And God did not promise me He would keep all the bad away from me; He promised me He would help me *through* it!

Often as Christians we want things to go perfectly for us once we say, God, I will follow you. That will not happen. If or when you choose to follow Christ, remember this scripture:

John 16:33

> *I have told you these things, so that in me you may have peace. In this world you will have trouble. But take heart! I have overcome the world.*

God does not simply take away our troubles when we come to him. He gives us what we need to get through the struggles.

I have often wondered, why Lord, why do these things happen? We ask questions like, why does my friend have cancer? Why can't I find a job? Why am I always sick? Why, why, why.

In Psalms 25:17, David longed for relief:

> *Relieve the troubles of my heart and free me from my anguish.*

Yet, there is something built in us when we go through hard times.

Romans 4:5 says,

We also rejoice in our sufferings, because we know that suffering produces perseverance; perseverance, character; and character, hope. And hope does not disappoint us, because God has poured out His love into our hearts through the Holy Spirit, whom He has given us....

James 1:12 says,

Blessed is the man who perseveres under trial, because when he has stood the test, he will receive the crown of life that God has promised to those who love Him.

4. Think back to the last struggle you went through. Can you think of a way it made you stronger, built character in you, or in the end allowed you to see the love of God?

Study Guide Chapter 6: The best things come to those who wait.
Isaiah 40:31 (NKJV)

But those who wait on the Lord

Shall renew their strength;

They shall mount up with wings like eagles,

They shall run and not be weary,

They shall walk and not faint.

Take a moment to think. Can you picture someone you know who prays? At my home church there is a group of ladies. They meet once a week downstairs in the fellowship hall. It is a group of seasoned ladies who have experienced and lived life. Those grannies (as they call themselves) are there to hang out and encourage one another, but they gather together for so much more than that. They are there to *pray*. Each week they lift up our pastoral team and families in prayer. They lift the sick and the broken of our church before the ultimate Healer, and they pray for the children and teens in our local schools. Why? Because they want to see God do something.

1. When was the last time you prayed about something and saw the Lord respond to your prayer?

2. Do you believe that prayer can change things? How often do you spend time in prayer for the things that matter?

3. What in your life do you need to spend time in prayer for?

4. Do you have a group of people whom you can ask for prayer? Who are they and how often do you take your needs to them?

5. When you pray, do you expect to see results? James 1:6 says, "But ask in faith, with no doubting, for the one who doubts is like a wave of the sea that is driven and tossed by the wind." Are you expecting God to answer you when you pray?

6. In Romans 10:1 the apostle Paul wrote, "Brothers, my heart's desire and prayer to God for them is that they may be saved." Paul had such a deep desire to see people know about Christ. Once we come to a place of deciding to follow Christ, the next thing to do is pray for others to find Jesus. The best things come to those who wait on the Lord—those who pray. Who in your world needs to be prayed for?

There is so much we can pray for: salvation, healing, and protection for our loved ones as well as our community. Take it to the next level and we will see the best things come to pass for those around us!

Study Guide Chapter 7: Flawless grace

Imago dei. The image of God. We were made to be like our Creator, made in His image, yet with each flaw we find on ourselves we somehow stop seeing His perfect reflection.

I came to Jesus hurting and broken. By the time I was getting ready to stand at the altar to be married, I was freaked out about how I was going to overcome the things in my life that stained me and made me gross. Here as a twenty-three-year-old woman I still felt dirty. It was at this time that I finally talked to a counselor. Teresa loved Jesus. She helped me see my value and probably saved my marriage before it even started. She showed me Jesus in a new way and I was then able to see that there was hope for me. Jesus fixed me up. He planted my feet back on solid ground! Then I saw grace.

We all have things we need to have covered by grace. Sometimes they are our own wrongdoings, and sometimes they are the fault of others. But no matter, they still mess us up and put holes in us.

1. In what area of your life do you need flawless grace?

2. What are you going to do to help yourself find that grace?

Jesus is my super hero. Jesus is my everything—my amazing grace, my flawless.

3. It is time to spend some time crying out to the Lord to find healing for the broken places. We need to putty the cracks of our lives with the healing balm of Jesus.

Flawless grace, I need it every day. His amazing, flawless grace covers my sin, my shame, my guilt, the wrongs done against me and my every pain. Let His flawless grace be enough for you.

Study Guide Chapter 8: To have a friend be a friend

Trust is something that can take years to build, but only moments to destroy. And honestly, betrayal sucks.

1. Have you ever trusted someone only to be stabbed in the back in return?

2. Is that friendship or relationship still intact or was it beyond repair?

3. If you still have that relationship in your life, how difficult was it to trust again?

Broken relationships and broken trust can destroy you! When we allow roots of bitterness and hatred or unresolved pain to lead our thoughts, the results can be disastrous.

As long as we have unresolved issues of hurt and betrayal in our lives, we cannot move on to the amazing things that God has for us. We need to forgive. Not to help the one who hurt us but to help ourselves.

Forgiveness doesn't excuse someone's behavior. Forgiveness keeps others behavior from destroying you.

It is that simple.

4. What areas of unresolved hurt do you have? Have you let the betrayal of someone deeply wound you?

There is a time for forgiveness and there is a time to move on. This does not necessarily mean that a restoration of the relationship will follow, but it also does not mean that full restoration is not possible.

If you have a relationship in jeopardy, one that has been a victim of betrayal, you may need to ask yourself a couple of questions:

1. Is the relationship safe for you if restored?

2. Is the relationship worth saving?

3. Does the other person in the relationship want to save the relationship?

When toxic friendships come into our lives they need to be handled with care. Often the only way to heal from this kind of relationship is to jump ship. If a friend continues to hurt you, you may need to let go of that friendship, and start praying for a new friend. It is amazing how some of the greatest friendships can come from the times in our life where we feel alone. Friendship is such a gift. So when you find a good one, cherish that friend. Make sure you are a good friend in return.

Study Guide Chapter 9: What doesn't kill you makes you stronger

These words cover so many areas of our lives. We constantly go through things that build character, strength, wisdom, and compassion in us.

Time to think deep

1. Is there someone in your world right now going through a season in their life that seems to be at the threshold of what they can handle?

2. Is there something you can do to support them in their time of need?

Or maybe you are the one facing the looming giant, not knowing how you will get through your circumstances.

Psalm 34:18-19 (NIV) says this:

> *The Lord is close to the brokenhearted*
>
> *and saves those who are crushed in spirit.*
>
> *The righteous person may have many troubles,*
>
> *but the Lord delivers him from them all.*

There is great hope here. Not only is God going to stick with me during my difficult times, but He is eventually going to deliver me from them. When we are wounded, fighting, and broken down, God does not abandon us.

Matthew 20:12 says,

A bruised reed he will not break, and a smoldering wick he will not snuff out, till he has brought justice through to victory.

God simply will not break us, abandon us, or snuff us out!

Yet we still find ourselves in precarious positions. We are insecure and unstable, teetering like we're on the top rung of a wobbly ladder. In the midst of the pain coming from the wounds we accumulate, and the fears that accompany our monsters in the closet, we hide. We don't count on Jesus to help us through and we don't turn to the people God has placed in our lives for support. Instead, we put on a mask and try to pretend that we are just fine.

What masks do you wear? Do you put on a mask of joy in the midst of sorrow? Do you wear a mask of contentment in the midst of the dissatisfaction you have in your circumstances?

3. What mask do you wear to make everyone think you are ok?

4. What deep pain are you dealing with in life that is threatening to overtake you?

5. What do you fear?

God wants to help you through it. He wants to meet you in your quiet, safe place and wrap His arms around you. Are you bruised? Is your fire about to go out? God is ready to straighten out and mend you; then He will ignite you. You have potential! You are loved. You do not need to hide your troubles so that you look perfect to the world. You can allow your troubles to be exposed to the light. Then you have the power, through the spirit of God, to help others like you and to light the world on fire!

What does not kill you makes you stronger! But only if you let it.

Remember the words of Jesus in John 16:33:

In this world you will have trouble. But take heart! I have overcome the world.

The key to overcoming trouble is Jesus. Cast your cares on him. He can handle it.

Study Guide Chapter 10: Mourning is allowed

I am sure I would have been a daddy's girl. I just never had the opportunity until the crucial moment of bonding had passed me by.

I am sure my life would have been different if there had been no Vietnam War.

I am sure that if I had never met Charles, I would have had a higher self-worth as a young person.

I am sure that if I didn't have learning disabilities, I would have thought I was smarter.

I am sure if I had felt beautiful as a young girl, I would not long to think that someone believes I am today.

Loss! Deprivation! Death of our self-worth. Theft of your childhood. These are things that need to be mourned.

What do you need to mourn?

Failed marriage

Loss of a child (by death or relationship)

Loss of a parent

Parent that was simply not present in your life

Loss of mobility

Loss of innocence

Loss of heart

1. What are the things in your life that you have lost? How has that loss affected you?

2. Have you ever mourned the loss of something besides a person? How does mourning look the same/different in that situation?

3. Have you ever experienced God restoring back to you what you have lost?

4. What does it mean to you that God can restore to you what you have lost? Does it give you hope for your future?

Restoration can take many forms. It can look very different in different situations. God wants to restore you. He wants you to live in the fullness of His joy.

David wrote Psalms 40 as he was being chased down. He fears for his life and his losses are great, yet he writes:

> *I waited patiently for the Lord;*
>
> *he turned to me and heard my cry.*
>
> *He lifted me out of the slimy pit,*
>
> *out of the mud and mire;*
>
> *he set my feet on a rock*
>
> *and gave me a firm place to stand.*
>
> *He put a new song in my mouth,*
>
> *a hymn of praise to our God.*
>
> *Many will see and fear the Lord*
>
> *and put their trust in him.*

Blessed is the one

who trusts in the Lord,

who does not look to the proud,

to those who turn aside to false gods.

Many, Lord my God,

are the wonders you have done,

the things you planned for us.

None can compare with you;

were I to speak and tell of your deeds,

they would be too many to declare.

The Lord has great things for you! You just have to trust him while he is putting it all into play.

Study Guide Chapter 11: Saying I am sorry

Sorry, such a sweet, simple little word. Or is it? Have you ever been in a place where you knew you were wrong but you did not want to apologize? Humility is rough sometimes. Those five letters are often the hardest ones to leave our mouths. Sometimes we overuse them, but more often than not we don't use them enough, or at the right times.

Yet there is such freedom in the words *I am sorry*.

There are two things I believe God wanted me to learn in the crawl space about the words *I am sorry*. First, live in humility and don't worry about the words making you look weak. Second, be quick to forgive others even if the words *I am sorry* are never spoken.

1. Who in your world do you need to forgive?

2. Is the bitterness that comes with lack of forgiveness hurting you or the person you hold the grudge toward?

3. What do you gain when you are quick to forgive?

I have seen people who say they forgave the wrongs that were done against them. I have seen people stand on a platform and declare how great God is, in bringing them through their circumstances, yet you can tell that they have never forgiven those who wronged them. They are lacking in freedom. Until we let go of the feelings of malice towards the ones who have wronged us, we cannot have the fullness of God's joy. We will without a doubt live a cup-half-empty life!

Forgiveness, what does the Bible say about that?

Matthew 6:14-15 ESV

For if you forgive others their trespasses, your heavenly Father will also forgive you, but if you do not forgive others their trespasses, neither will your Father forgive your trespasses.

Ephesians 4:32 ESV

Be kind to one another, tenderhearted, forgiving one another, as God in Christ forgave you.

Luke 17:3-4 ESV

Pay attention to yourselves! If your brother sins, rebuke him, and if he repents, forgive him, and if he sins against you seven times in the day, and turns to you seven times, saying, 'I repent,' you must forgive him.

Leviticus 19:18 ESV

You shall not take vengeance or bear a grudge against the sons of your own people, but you shall love your neighbor as yourself: I am the Lord.

Mark 11:25 ESV

And whenever you stand praying, forgive, if you have anything against anyone, so that your Father also who is in heaven may forgive you your trespasses."

Ephesians 4:26 ESV

Be angry and do not sin; do not let the sun go down on your anger

James 1:19-20 ESV

Know this, my beloved brothers: let every person be quick to hear, slow to speak, slow to anger; for the anger of man does not produce the righteousness of God.

Colossians 3:12-14 ESV

Put on then, as God's chosen ones, holy and beloved, compassionate hearts, kindness, humility, meekness, and patience, bearing with one another and, if one has a complaint against another, forgiving each other; as the Lord has forgiven you, so you also must forgive. And above all these put on love, which binds everything together in perfect harmony.

Ephesians 4:31 ESV

Let all bitterness and wrath and anger and clamor and slander be put away from you, along with all malice.

Proverbs 19:11 ESV

Good sense makes one slow to anger, and it is his glory to overlook an offense.

Matthew 18:21-22 ESV

Then Peter came up and said to him, "Lord, how often will my brother sin against me, and I forgive him? As many as seven times?" Jesus said to him, "I do not say to you seven times, but seventy times seven.

Colossians 3:13 ESV

Bearing with one another and, if one has a complaint against another, forgiving each other; as the Lord has forgiven you, so you also must forgive.

Luke 6:31 ESV

And as you wish that others would do to you, do so to them.

Matthew 5:7 ESV

Blessed are the merciful, for they shall receive mercy.

Ephesians 4:31-32 ESV

Let all bitterness and wrath and anger and clamor and slander be put away from you, along with all malice. Be kind to one another, tenderhearted, forgiving one another, as God in Christ forgave you.

James 2:8 ESV

If you really fulfill the royal law according to the Scripture, "You shall love your neighbor as yourself," you are doing well.

James 1:26 ESV

If anyone thinks he is religious and does not bridle his tongue but deceives his heart, this person's religion is worthless.

Romans 12:17-21 ESV

Repay no one evil for evil, but give thought to do what is honorable in the sight of all. If possible, so far as it depends on you, live peaceably with all. Beloved, never avenge yourselves, but leave it to the wrath of God, for it is written, "Vengeance is mine, I will repay, says the Lord." To the contrary, "if your enemy is hungry, feed him; if he is thirsty, give him something to drink; for by so doing you will heap burning coals on his head." Do not be overcome by evil, but overcome evil with good.

Matthew 7:12 ESV

So whatever you wish that others would do to you, do also to them, for this is the Law and the Prophets.

James 5:9 ESV

Do not grumble against one another, brothers, so that you may not be judged; behold, the Judge is standing at the door.

Colossians 3:8 ESV

But now you must put them all away: anger, wrath, malice, slander, and obscene talk from your mouth.

Romans 14:1 ESV

As for the one who is weak in faith, welcome him, but not to quarrel over opinions.

Romans 12:19 ESV

Beloved, never avenge yourselves, but leave it to the wrath of God, for it is written, "Vengeance is mine, I will repay, says the Lord."

Ephesians 4:26-27 ESV

Be angry and do not sin; do not let the sun go down on your anger, and give no opportunity to the devil.

Matthew 5:43-48 ESV

You have heard that it was said, 'You shall love your neighbor and hate your enemy.' But I say to you, Love your enemies and pray for those who persecute you, so that you may be sons of your Father who is in heaven. For he makes his sun rise on the evil and on the good, and sends rain on the just and on the unjust. For if you love those who love you, what reward do you have? Do not even the tax collectors do the same? And if you greet only your brothers, what more are you doing than others? Do not even the Gentiles do the same? ...

Matthew 5:5-9 ESV

Blessed are the meek, for they shall inherit the earth. Blessed are those who hunger and thirst for righteousness, for they shall be satisfied. Blessed are the merciful, for they shall receive mercy. Blessed are the pure in heart, for they shall see God. Blessed are the peacemakers, for they shall be called sons of God.

Proverbs 24:29 ESV

Do not say, "I will do to him as he has done to me; I will pay the man back for what he has done."

Proverbs 20:22 ESV

Do not say, "I will repay evil"; wait for the Lord, and he will deliver you.

Proverbs 12:16 ESV

The vexation of a fool is known at once, but the prudent ignores an insult.

1 John 3:14 ESV

We know that we have passed out of death into life, because we love the brothers. Whoever does not love abides in death.

1 Peter 4:8 ESV

Above all, keep loving one another earnestly, since love covers a multitude of sins.

James 1:2-4 ESV

Count it all joy, my brothers, when you meet trials of various kinds, for you know that the testing of your faith produces steadfastness. And let steadfastness have its full effect, that you may be perfect and complete, lacking in nothing.

Colossians 3:14 ESV

And above all these put on love, which binds everything together in perfect harmony.

Colossians 3:7-8 ESV

In these you too once walked, when you were living in them. But now you must put them all away: anger, wrath, malice, slander, and obscene talk from your mouth.

Whoa . . . hold the phone, that is a lot of verses.

Okay, so maybe I went a little overboard on the collection here. I could have gone on and on. The message here is overwhelming. Forgive others! It is God's command to us.

By allowing yourself to forgive and be forgiven, you accept the freedom that comes with it. Be quick to accept your mistakes and be quick to say "I'm sorry." But also be quick to forgive those who have wronged you. The day I decided to forgive my father I found freedom, and the day I forgave Charles my abuser, I found freedom. Through my life I have had to forgive many times as I found myself hurt deeply by others. Now you need to forgive, for there is freedom found there.

4. What is it that keeps us from forgiving others?

5. What is it that keeps us from saying *I am sorry*?

6. What do you need to do to get to the place where you have freedom through forgiveness in every area of your life?

Don't be afraid to say *I am sorry* and don't let bitterness keep you from forgiving others.

Study Guide Chapter 12: Forgive yourself

Forgiving oneself is often the hardest thing we have to do. I know of an acquaintance of mine who lost a child several years ago. They had an in-ground pool in their back yard, and while the mother was away at the store, the father lost track of the two-and-a-half-year-old child. The child drowned.

I know of another family whom I have not met, only heard the story through a member of my family, who once again, while the mother was not home and the children were out in the yard playing in a leaf pile on the side of the road, the father ran inside the house to get a camera, and while the father was inside the house the children were struck by a car and killed.

Tragedy struck both of these families and I can only imagine the feelings of guilt inside these two fathers. Tragic circumstances overwhelmed them. Did they wish for those tragic deaths? Absolutely not! I am absolutely sure these two dads would do anything they could to reverse what happened, but of course that is impossible.

I have talked to people who have, in moments of weakness, cheated on their spouses, and I met a woman at Safeway several years ago who was soon headed to prison because while she was on her phone, she struck a pedestrian and the person died. The woman was facing years of prison for vehicular manslaughter. Though a little different than the above stories, these people's bad choices also created the tragedy at hand.

What do all of the people involved in these tragedies have in common? Each one of them lives with immense guilt. They each feel responsible for a tragedy.

Life is so hard sometimes. There are happenings in and out of our hands that cause great turmoil within us. I do not have such a tragic story as these; however, I have had times where I have caused or been near a situation where I didn't try to stop it, and bad things happened. I have said the wrong things and caused others pain and I've made bad decisions that brought me guilt.

Forgiving yourself is one of the hardest things you may ever have to do.

1. Is there a time in your life where you caused someone pain and you are having a hard time forgiving yourself?

2. Do you know of someone who has wronged you and you have forgiven them but you know they have not forgiven themselves?

Forgiveness = freedom, as we discovered in the last chapter, but when it is me I need to forgive, it is much more difficult.

How do I move on and forgive myself when I am stuck in my own self-pity?

3. Have you said *I am sorry* to the person you may have wronged?

4. Have you talked to Jesus about your feelings of guilt?

Freedom can be yours when you begin to see forgiveness for what it is.

What is forgiveness?   Forgiveness is a conscious, deliberate decision, to release feelings of resentment or vengeance toward someone. Forgiveness is not denial. It is not saying you are not responsible for wrongdoings. Forgiveness is consciously deciding not to let it eat you alive.

Christ died to give us forgiveness. You just need to accept it.

Study Guide Chapter 13: The most debilitating disability in life is a bad attitude

Labels, they are everywhere. You are autistic. She is dyslexic. He is paraplegic. She is blind. We walk around as if we have words painted on our forehead signifying our disabilities. Yet I know paralyzed people impacting the world. Some of the smartest people I know are autistic, and dyslexic.

The true disability comes to us when we decide that we are going to let our disabilities keep us from our dreams.

I know too many people who do not have disabilities who are not living up to the potential of what they can be.

Attitude is everything!

1. What do these words mean to you?

2. What disabilities have you had to overcome?

3. How have the disabilities in your life helped you become who you are?

4. How do they inspire you to help others?

Impossibilities become possibilities when we have confidence, when we believe in ourselves and when we allow God to do great things through us. When we begin to focus on the power of God rather than how daunting our own problems are, we begin do great things.

Before we can overcome our physical disabilities, we have to overcome the obstacles that are in our minds. We have to also believe that with God we can overcome any and every obstacle we face. If we are in pain, such as those who suffer from fibromyalgia, migraines, arthritis, or even the phantom pain of an amputation, it is hard to see past your handicap. Depression and anxiety can come into play and you suddenly feel even more crippled.

I am in no way trying to downplay the very real, very debilitating actuality of these infirmities. Yet I want to offer hope that you can overcome, that you can accomplish great things. You are strong even in your weakness. It is in our weakness that we genuinely rely on God's strength.

5. What is it that you need to do to trust God in the middle of your infirmities?

6. According to Psalm 28:7, where does our strength come from?

7. 2 Corinthians 12:9-10 (NLT) says,

My grace is all you need. My power works best in weakness. So now I am glad to boast about my weaknesses, so that the power of Christ can work through me. That's why I take pleasure in my weaknesses and in the insults, hardships, persecutions, and troubles that I suffer for Christ. For when I am weak, then I am strong.

According to this scripture, how do our disabilities make us stronger than ever?

Depression, anxiety, fibromyalgia, arthritis, psoriasis, and so many other things cripple us. But in our weakness, He is made strong. His grace is enough for me. I will overcome. I will be strong and I will lead others to the One from whom my strength comes. It is all in our attitude.

I was able to overcome my learning disabilities, but it is hard to come out on top with a bad attitude. Bad attitudes simply compound problems. What are the attitudes holding you back? Let them roll like water off a ducks back! You hold the power to having a better day. Attitude is everything!

Study Guide Chapter 14: We are here to make a difference

I am here to make a difference. So are you!

We all have a story. We were not meant to hide it.

1. What is your story? Take some time and write it out. What have you learned from the pages of this book?

2. How can you use it? How can your story help someone?

3. We all have a crawl space of some kind. What are the lessons you learned in yours?

It is your turn to shine. How will you grow from your story? Share your story. I hope you have been inspired by my lessons from the crawl space! Now it is time to find peace with your own story. Who knows what person's life is out there just waiting for your story to be a catalyst for life change?

Learn from your crawl space

Go change the world

Study Guide Chapter 15: Be someone who cares

Have you ever wondered if you could really make a difference? What do you think it is that keeps people from trying to care for other people in need? Is it the fear that we will do it wrong, or won't have the right words to say? Maybe we don't engage with others because we worry about rejection. Maybe insecurity about our own worthiness gets in our way. Whatever the reason, it is time to take a new direction in life! It is time to be someone who genuinely cares!

Look around you.

1. Who in your world simply needs to know someone cares?

2. Whose life can you make a difference in?

We all have gifts, talents, and stories. Yours can definitely be used to help show someone that they are cared about. No matter how big or small you view your inadequacy, God sees it as possibility!

SO... What are your gifts?

Are you a baker? Maybe your elderly neighbor doesn't get a lot of visitors. Maybe a batch of cookies would brighten his day.

Are you a mechanic? Maybe the single mom at church needs an oil change and just offering to do it may be the act of kindness that shows her there is hope.

Are you a seamstress? Make something. Are you an encourager? Encourage!

3. What are the gifts or talents you have that you can use to change a life?

4. Who is someone you can bless this week and how?

Can you remember a time when someone blessed you?

5. How did it feel to know they cared?

Matthew 5:14-16 says,

You are the world's light—a city on a hill, glowing in the night for all to see. Don't hide your light! Let it shine for all; let your good deeds glow for all to see, so that they will praise your heavenly Father.

The kindness we show to others lets them know we care. When we care, we are a light.

Be someone who cares.

About the author—

Amy Johnson is a pastor and counselor who resides in a rural Washington town, where she enjoys life with her husband and three children. Active in ministry and in the community, she wants to make a difference in all she does. Amy feels called to speak into the lives of people who have experienced circumstances that are not easily overcome. She loves working with the students in her community, and serves as a children's minister and director of a student's theatre program. Writing books that encourage others has been a life goal for Amy, and she is currently writing her first inspirational novel titled *It Is Well*. Look for it soon on Amazon.

Made in the USA
San Bernardino, CA
29 September 2017